I0168879

Reuben Archer Torrey

Ought Christians to keep the Sabbath

Reuben Archer Torrey

Ought Christians to keep the Sabbath

ISBN/EAN: 9783337865214

Printed in Europe, USA, Canada, Australia, Japan

Cover: Foto ©Lupo / pixelio.de

More available books at **www.hansebooks.com**

OUGHT CHRISTIANS TO KEEP THE SABBATH?"

By: R. A. TORREY

Fleming H. Revell Company
New York Chicago Toronto

Publishers of Evangelical Literature

Copyrighted 1899, by Fleming H. Revell Company

INTRODUCTION.

Before reading this tract upon one of the burning questions of the day, the reader is earnestly requested to go to God in prayer and covenant with Him that he will take his stand upon what the Word of God teaches, whether it may agree with his previous notions or not. Let us, at all cost, be true to the Word of God.

Having made this agreement with God, read the tract, Bible in hand, and read it to the end.

"Ought Christians to Keep the Sabbath?"

"The Sabbath was made for man and not man for the Sabbath: so that the Son of Man is Lord even of the Sabbath". Mark 2:27, 28, Revised Version.

There was nothing for which the religious leaders of Christ's day, the Pharisees, were such sticklers as the Sabbath. Everything must give way to the demands of the Sabbath law and their interpretation of it. Sabbath keeping was more important to their minds than love or mercy or the needs of man. (Matthew 12:7, 8.) Whatever a man might be or do that was good, if he did not keep the Sabbath according to their idea of it, he deserved to die and be damned. Sabbath keeping was the sum of all righteousness and Sabbath breaking was the sum of all wickedness. They pronounced Jesus Christ, the Son of God Himself, to be worthy of death because He did not keep the Sabbath in their way. (John 5:18.) The most constant conflict that Jesus had with the Jews was on the subject of Sabbath keeping. In bringing one of these conflicts to a close, He uttered the words of our text and declared the great underlying principles of the question. These are two. First, that the Sabbath was made for man and that man therefore is not to be sacrificed to Sabbath keeping, but Sabbath keeping to be made subservient to man's needs. Second, that the Son of Man - Jesus Christ - is Lord even of the Sabbath, and therefore has authority to modify it, change it, or abrogate it as He will.

This same Sabbath question is coming to the front in our day. Those old time Pharisees have their lineal descendants in the present day Seventh Day Adventists. To them also Sabbath keeping is the sum of all righteousness and Sabbath breaking, according to their interpretation of it, i.e., the keeping of the first day of the week, instead of the seventh day of the week, is the sum of all wickedness, "the mark of the beast, "as they put it. Wherever the word "commandment" is used in the New Testament they read in the word fourth or Sabbath, thus corrupting the Word of God by adding to it what the Holy Spirit has not said. (Revelation 22: 18.) For example, one of their valiant warriors wrote me a letter, quoting 1 John 2:4, "He that saith, I know Him and keepeth not His commandments is a liar, and the truth is not in him, "and he wrote it this way, "He that saith, I know Him and keepeth not His (Sabbath) commandment is a liar, and the truth is not in him. "When I showed him it did not so read and the Holy Ghost had taken pains to say what commandments he meant in the next chapter, verse 23, "This is His commandment, that ye should believe on the name of His Son Jesus Christ and love one another as He gave us commandment"(1 John 3:23), he simply balked back in the harness and refused to retract.

The Seventh Day Adventists are very fond of making a similar use of Revelation 22:18, "Blessed are they that do His commandments, that they may have right to the tree of life and may enter in through the gates into the city. "This is one of their favorite passages, and they make the commandments here to mean the ten commandments, and especially the fourth. Not only is there no hint that the ten commandments are meant, but anyone who will take the pains to look up the Revised Version will find that all reference to any commandments has disappeared in the text, and the text reads, as it ought, "Blessed are they that wash their robes, that they may have the right to come to the tree of life, and may enter in by the gates into the city." Perhaps some early day legalist, like our modern Seventh Day Adventist, was not satisfied with the Word of God as it read and substituted the law for the Gospel.

These successors of the Pharisees of Jesus' day and Judaizers of Paul's day are seeking to break up the churches on this question. They are sending their missionaries and their books and tracts everywhere; they are using the most subtle and oftentimes underhand methods to get people under the yoke of the law In a word, they are repeating the tactics a3 well as the errors of those Judaizers whom Paul so strongly rebukes in his Epistle to the Galatians. They zealously seek weak and uninstructed Christians in no good way, nay, they desire to shut them out, that they may seek them. (Galatians 4:17, Revised Version) Like the young Christians in Galatia, many are being un- settled and drifting into legalism in this way. Just as the question "Ought Christians to be circumcised after the manner of Moses "was a burning and important one in Paul's day (Acts 15:1-29; Galatians 1:6, 7; 2:4-16; 3:1-29; 4:21-31; 5:1-4) so the question "Ought Christians to keep the Sabbath "is a burning and important one today. I take it up this morning to set some free from the yoke of bondage who have become entangled in it and to help others to stand fast in the liberty wherewith Christ has made them free. (Galatians 5:1.)

We will study the question from the Bible. We will find what the scripture saith. In order that we may clearly grasp it and hold it we will put the scripture teaching in a series of plain, unanswerable propositions and thus we will proceed step by step surely.

I. The first proposition is this: THE Sabbath as a law is a distinctly Jewish institution. Deuteronomy 5:12-15, "Keep the sabbath day to sanctify it, as the Lord thy God hath commanded thee. Six days shalt thou labor, and do all thy work: but the seventh day is the sabbath of the Lord thy God ; in it thou shalt not do any work, thou, nor thy son, nor thy daughter, nor thy manservant, nor thy maidservant, nor thine ox, nor thine ass, nor any oi thy cattle, nor thy stranger that is within thy gates; that thy manservant and thy maidservant may rest as well as thou. And remember that thou wast a servant in the land of Egypt, and that the LORD thy God brought thee out hence through a mighty hand and by a stretched-out arm: therefore, the LORD thy God commanded thee to keep the sabbath day." If you look to the other place where the ten commandments are given, (Exodus 20) they are prefaced in this way, "And God spake all these words, saying, I am the Lord thy God, which have brought thee out of the land of Egypt, out of the house of bondage," Exodus 20:1, 2. So the ten commandments in the form given are distinctly said to be for the Israelite. The moral principles underlying them are eternal and every one of them except the Sabbath commandment, as we shall see later, is reaffirmed in the New Testament. Look again to Exodus 31:13-17, "Speak thou also unto the children of Israel, saying, Verily my sabbaths ye shall keep: for it is a sign between me and you throughout your generations; that ye may know that I am the Lord that doth sanctify you. Ye shall keep the sabbath therefore; for it is holy unto you: everyone that defileth it shall surely be put to death: for whosoever doeth any work therein, that soul shall be cut off from among his people. Six days may work be done; but in the seventh is the sabbath of rest, holy to the Lord: whosoever doeth any work in the sabbath day, he shall surely be put to death. Wherefore the children of Israel shall keep the sabbath, to observe the Sabbath throughout their generations, for a perpetual covenant. It is a sign between me and the children of Israel forever; for in six days the Lord made heaven and earth, and on the seventh day he rested, and was refreshed. "We see this still again in Ezekiel 20:12, 13, "Moreover also I gave them my sabbaths, to be a sign between me and them that they might know that I am the Lord that sanctify them. But the house of Israel rebelled against me in the wilderness : they walked not in my statutes, and they despised my judgments, which if a man do, he shall even live in them; and my sabbaths they greatly polluted: then I said, I would pour out my fury upon them in the wilderness, to consume them. "Over and over again it is clearly stated in the Bible that the Sabbath as given in the law is a sign between God and the children of Israel. The sabbath as given in the ten commandments is a distinctly Jewish institution. We do not need to enter into the much disputed question whether the Sabbath was kept in the times between Eden and Sinai for we are concerned simply with the Sabbath law as found in the ten commandments; for it is necessarily upon this that the Seventh Day people rest the weight of their argument, and both when that law is given at Sinai and when it is repeated in Deuteronomy and in after comments upon it, it is distinctly said to be a law for Israel. It is true that when the work of creation was ended "God blessed the seventh day, and sanctified it; because that in it He had rested from all His work which God had created and made, "Gen. 2:3, but He did not give it there as a law, and where it is given as a law, as we have already seen, it is distinctly said to be a law for Israel. We would naturally expect if this is the case that in the times to come when God will again deal with Israel as a nation that the Sabbath would be brought forward again. And this is precisely what we find. Isaiah 56:2-7, "Blessed is the man that doeth this, and the son of man that layeth hold on it; that keepeth the sabbath from polluting it, and keepeth his hand from doing any evil. Neither let the son of the stranger that hath joined himself, to the Lord, speak, saying, The Lord hath utterly separated me from his people: neither let the eunuch say, Behold, lam a dry tree. For thus saith the Lord unto the eunuchs that keep my sabbaths, and choose the things that please me, and take hold of my covenant; even unto them will I give in mine house and within my walls a place and a name better than of sons and of daughters: I will give them an everlasting name, that shall not be cut off. Also the sons of the stranger, that join themselves to the Lord, to serve him, and to love the name of the Lord, to be his servants, every one that keepeth the Sabbath from polluting it and taketh hold of my covenant; even them will I bring to my holy mountain, and make them joyful in. my house of prayer; their burnt offerings and their sacrifices shall be accepted upon mine altar; for mine house shall be called an house of prayer for all people"; Isaiah 58:12,13, "And they that shall be of thee shall build the old waste places : thou shalt raise up the foundations of many generations; and thou shalt be called, The repairer of the breach, The restorer of paths to dwell in, If thou turn away thy foot from the sabbath, from doing thy pleasure on my holy day; and call the sabbath a delight. the holy of the Lord, honorable; and shalt honor him, not doing thine own ways, nor finding thine own pleasure nor speaking thine own words"; Isaiah 66:22,23, "For as the new heavens and the new earth, which I will make, shall remain before me, saith the Lord, so shall your seed and your name remain. And it shall come to pass, that from one new moon to another, and from one sabbath to another, shall all flesh come to worship before me, saith the Lord"; Ezekiel 46:1-3, "Thus saith the Lord God: The gate of the inner court that looketh toward the east shall be shut the six work in g days; but on the sabbath it shall be opened, and in the day of the new moon it shall be opened. And the prince shall enter by the way of the porch of that gate without, and shall stand by the post of the gate, and the priests shall prepare his burnt offering and his peace offerings, and he shall worship at the threshold of the gate: then he shall go forth; but the gate shall not be shut until the evening. Likewise, the people of the land shall worship at the door of this gate before the Lord in the sabbaths and in the new moons. "All these passages as the context clearly shows have to do with the times to come, the future Jewish times, when God shall again deal with Israel and the Sabbath and other features of the Jewish ceremonial be restored. When the church times are ended and Israelitish times taken up again, the sabbath will be renewed for Israel. The Seventh Day Adventists are constantly overlooking one of the fundamental principles of Biblical interpretation, that we must distinguish between the Jew, the Gentile and the church of God. (1 Corinthians 10:32.) And the other fundamental principle of biblical interpretation closely connected with this, that there are in the Bible Jewish times and church times. "When God dealt with Israel we were in Jewish times, but the Jew has been laid aside for a time and we are now in the times of the Gentiles (Romans 11: 25; Luke 21: 24) and church times. When the church shall be complete and caught up to meet her Lord in the air and the times of the Gentiles shall be fulfilled, then God will begin to deal with Israel again and Jewish times recommence and the Sabbath, which is a Jewish institution, will be restored. It is a remarkable and significant fact that the prophetic passages given above upon which the Seventh Day Adventists lay so much stress are clearly stated to belong to those times when God again deals with Israel in mercy. It is evident that the Sabbath as a law is a distinctly Jewish institution.

II. The second proposition is that the law written and engraven on stones - which of course includes the Sabbath law - is done away. This the Scriptures affirm in the most positive way. 2 Corinthians 3:7-11, "But if the ministration of death, written and engraven in stones, was glorious, so that the children of Israel could not steadfastly behold the face of Moses for the glory of his countenance; which glory was to be done away: How shall not the ministration of the spirit be rather glorious? For if the ministration of condemnation be glory, much more doth the ministration of righteousness exceed in glory. For even that which was made glorious had no glory in this respect, by reason of the glory that excelleth. For if that which is done away was glorious, much more that which remaineth is glorious. "Could anything be plainer than that? The Seventh Day Adventist asks you, was not the Sabbath law on the tables of stone, and he thinks it is a knock-down argument. So it is, but it knocks down the wrong party, the Seventh Day Adventist himself, for we are told that the law engraven on stones, so far from being binding on us, is done away.

The Seventh Day Adventist seeks to avoid the force of this by saying that in the passage quoted it is "the glory "that was done away and not the law itself. This may be said about the seventh verse, but in the eleventh verse we are told that it was that which was "with glory"(see Revised Version) that was done away, that is, it was the law itself which was done away. So, this refuge of the Seventh Day Adventist is annihilated. But someone will ask if the law written and engraven on stones was done away, what obligation are we under not to steal or murder or commit adultery or do any of the other things that are forbidden in the ten commandments. We shall see God's answer to this question presently. But let us hold to the point and settle one thing at a time. That one thing that we have now settled is that the law written and engraven on stones, including the Sabbath law, has no claim whatever on the Christian. In fact, is "done away. "We must stand by this position because the Spirit of God says so in the Word. It may not fit into our theories, but we must make our theories fit the Word of God, and not the Word of God our theories. The Seventh Day people are fond of telling us that the ceremonial law was done away, but the moral law, the ten commandments, still stands. But the Holy Spirit has guarded against this misinterpretation of scripture by telling us plainly that it was the law engraven on stones, the very part the Seventh Day people say stands, that was done away.

This same truth is put in another way in Romans 10:3-9, "For they being ignorant of God's righteousness, and going about to establish their own righteousness, have not submitted themselves unto the righteousness of God. For Christ is the end of the law for righteousness to everyone that believeth. For Moses describeth the righteousness, which is of the law, that the man which doeth those things shall live by them. But the righteousness, which is of faith speaketh on this wise, say not in thine heart, Who shall ascend into heaven? (that is, to bring Christ down from above:) or, who shall descend into the deep? (that is, to bring up Christ again from the dead.) But what saith it? The word is nigh thee, even in thy mouth, and in thy heart: that is, the word of faith, which we preach: That if thou shalt confess with thy mouth the Lord Jesus, and shalt believe in thine heart that God hath raised him from the dead, thou shalt be saved. "Oh, if these legalists could only get this fundamental principle of the Gospel, that Christ is the end of the law, fixed in their minds.

III. The third proposition is closely akin to the second. It is that Christians ARE BECOME DEAD TO THE LAW OF MOSES by the body of Christ. This is distinctly affirmed in Romans 7:1-4, "Know ye not, brethren (for I speak to them that know the law), how that the law hath dominion over a man as long as he liveth? For the woman which hath an husband is bound by the law to her husband as long as he liveth; but if the husband be dead, she is loosed from the law of her husband. So then if, while her husband liveth, she be married to another man, she shall be called an adulteress: but if her husband be dead, she is free from that law; so that she is no adulteress, though she be married to another man. Wherefore, my brethren, ye also are become dead to the law by the body of Christ; that ye should be married to another, even to him who is raised from the dead, that we should bring forth fruit unto God. "Paul distinctly affirms that the law of Moses has no more claim upon a Christian than a dead husband has upon a wife. We are married to another, even Christ, and by our union with Him and not by our obedience to the Mosaic law we bring forth fruit unto God.

IV. The fourth proposition is that the commandment that Jesus Christ lays up on us is not that we keep the sabbath, but that we love one another. John 13:34, "A new commandment I give unto you, that ye love one another; as I have loved you, that ye also love one another. "1 John 2:7-10, "Brethren, I write no new commandment unto you, but an old commandment which ye had from the beginning. The old commandment is the word which ye have had from the beginning. Again, a new commandment I write unto you, which thing is true in him and in you: because the darkness is past, and the true light now shineth. He that saith he is in the light, and hateth his brother, is in darkness even until now. He that loveth his brother abideth in the light, and there is none occasion of stumbling in him. "This latter passage is in immediate connection with the passage, where we are told that we prove that we know Him by keeping His commandment, and which the Seventh Day people constantly interpret to mean the Sabbath commandment, though the Holy Spirit distinctly says it is the commandment to love our brethren. Look also at 1 John 3:22-23, "And whatsoever we ask, we receive of him, because we keep his commandments, and do those things that are pleasing in his sight. And this is his commandment, that we should believe on the name of his Son Jesus Christ, and love one another, as he gave us commandment. "Love, not Sabbath-keeping, is the law of Christ. (Galatians 6:2.)

V. The fifth proposition is that every one of the Ten Commandments is expressly reaffirmed in the New Testament except the sabbath law, and there is not one syllable in our whole New Testament suggesting that the Sabbath is binding on the Christian. Look at Romans 13:8-10, "Owe no man anything, but to love one another: for he that loveth another hath fulfilled the law. For this, Thou shalt not commit adultery, Thou shalt not kill, Thou shalt not steal, Thou shalt not bear false witness, Thou shalt not covet; and if there be any other commandment, it is briefly comprehended in this saying, namely, Thou shalt love thy neighbor as thyself. Love worketh no ill to his neighbor: therefore, love is the fulfilling of the law." Here five commandments are reaffirmed, not because they were given by Moses, but because they grow out of the law of love, which is the law of Christ. The command to honor parents is declared binding on Christians in Ephesians 6:1, 2, "Children, obey your parents in the Lord: for this is right. Honor thy father and mother; which is the first commandment with promise. "The command not to take the name of God in vain is reaffirmed and amplified in James 5:12, "But above all things, my brethren, swear not, neither by heaven, neither by the earth, neither by any other oath: but let your yea be yea; and your nay, nay; lest ye fall into condemnation. "The command to have no other gods before God and not to worship images, is reaffirmed in 1 John 5:21, "Little children, keep yourselves from idols," and elsewhere. Every commandment, then, written on the tables of stone but the Sabbath law is explicitly declared in the New Testament to be binding on Christians. But the one commandment upon which the Seventh Day people lay all their emphasis is neither by explicit statement nor hint said to be binding upon Christians in any verse in the New Testament.

VI. The sixth proposition is more conclusive than any yet. Indeed, it is absolutely decisive. The Sabbath obligation is plainly and explicitly and unmistakably declared not to be binding upon the Christian. There is nothing in the whole New Testament plainer than this. Look at Colossians 2:16, 17: "Let no man therefore judge you in meat, or in drink, or in respect of an holy day, or of the new moon, or of the sabbath days; which are a shadow of things to come; but the body is of Christ. "I challenge any man to deal honestly and frankly with that passage and still claim that the Sabbath is binding on a Christian, I have given that to man after man who tried to maintain in conversation or correspondence this obligation of the Sabbath as resting upon a Christian. The best answer they could give is that

Paul here when he said Sabbath did not mean Sabbath in the ordinary sense, but other festival days of the Jewish year that were kept as Sabbaths. If Paul didn't mean Sabbath, why did he say Sabbath? There are three things that prove to a demonstration that Paul did mean the weekly Jewish seventh-day Sabbath. First, the word translated Sabbath, in this passage is never used in any passage in the New Testament of any day but the weekly Sabbath. Of course the same word might mean a week, but it is never wed of any day in the week, or any day in the year, or any other day, in the new Testament except of the weekly Sabbath; and so it can not mean any other day here. Second, that Paul did not mean some of the other feast days is clearly shown by the fact that in this very verse he distinctly distinguishes a feast day or a new moon from a Sabbath day. (See Revised Version) In the third place the very formula that Paul uses here, "a feast day or a new moon or a sabbath day" (Revised Version) is the regular formula used in the Old Testament for the set feasts, new moons and weekly Sabbaths. (See 2 Chronicles 1:4.) "On the sabbaths, and on the new moons, and on the solemn feasts of the Lord our God, "and 2 Chronicles 8:13, "On the sabbaths, and on the new moons, and on the solemn feasts, three times in the year, even in the feast of unleavened bread, and in the feast of weeks, and in the feast of tabernacles. "By a comparison with Numbers 28:9,11,16,19,26, we see that the Sabbaths here meant are the weekly Sabbaths, for this is the precise division of this chapter, "the set feasts, the new moons, and the weekly sabbath. "No man can frankly face Colossians 2:16, 17 and interpret it in the light of other scripture and come to any other conclusion than the Sabbath Paul mentions as having no binding force upon the Christian is the weekly Sabbath. This is what the Holy Spirit means in this passage, I bow to His authority and declare the Sabbath has no binding authority on the believer in Jesus Christ.

VII. The seventh proposition is that the Christian is on resurrection ground, and the natural and proper day for him to keep is the resurrection day, the first day of the week, the Lord's day. In Colossians 3: 1, we are told that we are risen with Christ, so we are on resurrection ground. We see the same thing in Romans 7:4, where we are expressly said to be set free from the Mosaic law. We see it everywhere in the New Testament after the resurrection of Christ. The seventh-day Sabbath belongs to the old creation; the first day, Lord's day, be- longs to the new creation. If one belongs to the old creation, let him keep the Sabbath; if he belongs to the new creation, let him keep the first day, the Lord's day. As I have gone on up to this point some may have thought, have we no Sabbath at all? We have not, as a matter of law. We have, as a matter of privilege, and not so much a Sabbath as a Lord's day. In the Sabbath, rest is the predominating idea. In the Lord's day, resurrection activity, spiritual work is the predominating idea. Each of the ten commandments is an expression of an eternal principle, and the eternal principle stands under the new dispensation as well as under the old. The great underlying thought of the fourth commandment is man's need of physical rest and spiritual refreshment. The Sabbath was made for man. It was meant to subserve a need of man. In the Lord's day that need is met in a higher way, and, it is not law now, but privilege. "The sabbath was made for man and not man for the sabbath," Mark 2:27. But, though it is privilege and not law, woe be to the man who despises his privilege. He will suffer. Woe be to the man who makes this day of holy privilege a day of secular activity, of work or hilarity or amusement, and forgets he has a soul to refresh by the study of the "Word of God and prayer and work for Christ. No man can despise the Lord's day with its holy privileges, without suffering grievously in spirit, soul and body. But the Christian will not keep the Lord's day in the bondage of a servant under law, but in the joyous liberty of a child of God.

But, as a matter of historic fact, did the early Christians keep the first day of the week In Acts 20:7 we are told that it was on the first day that the disciples came together to break bread. In 1 Corinthians 16;12 we are told the first day of the week the disciples were to set by their offerings. In Revelation 1:10 "the Lord's day "is expressly spoken of. Some of the Seventh Day Adventists would have us think that the Lord's day in Revelation 1:10 means the Sabbath, but it can be proven beyond a doubt to mean the first day of the week. Ignatius, who was himself a disciple of that John who tells us he was "in the Spirit of the Lord's day," wrote about 100 A. D., only a few years after John wrote. He says: "Those who were concerned with old things have come to newness of confidence, no longer keeping sabbaths, but living according to the Lord s day, on which our life as risen again through Him depends." "But," does someone say, "did not Paul keep the seventh day? Does it not say, for example, in Acts 17:3 that 'Paul, as his manner was, went in unto them, and three sabbath days reasoned with them out of the scriptures'?" It does, but Paul was working among Jews and that was the day they came together, and every Jewish missionary, today, works with them on Saturday, or the Sabbath, as that is the day you can reach them. Moreover, the early Gentile converts were under Jewish influence and Paul took them as he could get them, which was largely on the Sabbath. But when they were converted, they came together as Christians to break bread on the first day of the week. (Acts 20:7.) Much is made of the fact that Paul at Philippi went out on the Sabbath to the riverside. The explanation is very evident. There were Jews and Jewish proselytes who resorted, on the Sabbath, to the riverside and Paul began his work with them just as he did in other cities, and of course met with them at the time they were accustomed to meet. There can be no question what day God favored in those olden times after Jesus had risen. It was on the first day of the week Jesus appeared to Mary and Peter. (John 20 :1,14; Luke 24:34.) It was - on the first day He opened the minds of the two on the way to Emmaus to understand the Scriptures. (Luke 24:1, 13-35.) It was on the first day of the week that He appeared unto the ten, Thomas being absent, and breathed on them and said, "Receive ye the Holy Ghost." (John 20:19-23.) It was on the Lord's day, the first day of the week, He appealed again, Thomas being present. (John 20:26-29.) It was on the first day of the week, "Pentecost," that the Holy Ghost was given, three thousand converted and the church instituted. It was on the first day of the week that Jesus appeared to John in glory on Patmos. God, in every imaginable way, in those New Testament times set His seal on the first day of the week.

Even in the Old Testament in type the first day of the week was set forth as the day which in church times should supersede the seventh day. The sheaf of first fruits, the plain type of the Risen Christ (1 Corinthians 15:20) was presented on the first day of the week. (Lev. 23:9-11.) So also, Pentecost, the type of the church's offering, was to be on the first day of the week the morrow after the perfect cycle of seven Sabbaths was ended. (Lev. 23:15-17.) So, we see that even in the Old Testament there was a foreshadowing of the fact that in the resurrection days, in church times, the seventh day was to be superseded by the first. The first day of the week is the day on which God plainly set His seal as the church day, the day of a Risen Christ and a Risen Church.

VIII. Thus far we have appealed only to scripture, and we have clearly seen that not only is the seventh-day Sabbath not commanded in the Bible for the Christian but distinctly abrogated, and God has set His seal on the first day, or Lord's day, for the church. Now simply by way of confirmation from experience. I stand absolutely on scripture, but when experience confirms scripture so much the better. In the Bible we saw God set His seal on the first day. He is doing exactly the same thing in present day experience God is setting his seal on first day observance. When is the Holy Spirit most often, most manifestly and most abundantly poured out? I say without hesitation, on the first day of the week The Seventh Day people are a conscientious, zealous, self-sacrificing people, but there is among them a most noticeable lack of Holy Ghost joyousness, freedom and power. They are without liberty in life and without power in service. They are in bondage and in impotence. We would put the same question to them that Paul put to the Galatians when they too fell into legalism, "Received ye the Spirit by the works of the law, or by the hearing of faith, "Galatians 3:2. They are manifestly devoid of Holy Ghost experience and power. I have put this to man after man who has gone over to them and they have admitted it. They are not saving the lost but proselyting among those who are already saved. I put this to one of their most prominent and aggressive men and he said frankly, "Mr. Torrey, 1 admit you are right about that. That is our great fault. "They feel it themselves and are trying to remove this reproach by establishing missions to reach the lost. But how often they have to go to those whom God has honored as keepers of the first day to have their missions manned with men of power. God does not set the seal of His approval on seventh day ism, or legalism, by giving the Holy Spirit to them. He does set the seal of His approval on first dayism, or the renunciation of legalism, by giving His Spirit. Scripture and experience unite in condemning Sabbathism or legalism. It has absolutely no footing.

Let me add one word. The Seventh Day people either ignorantly or deliberately falsify history. They say we owe the first day keeping to the times of Constantine and a decree of the Pope or Roman Catholic church. This is a bald falsehood.

Ignatius, a disciple of John, about 100 A.D., says, "Those who were concerned with old things have come to newness of confidence, no longer keeping Sabbaths but living according to the Lord's day, on which our life as risen again through Him depends. "

Barnabas, in a letter that goes back almost to Apostolic times, says, "We keep the eighth day with Joy, on which day Jesus also arose from the dead, and having appeared, He ascended into Heaven. "

Justin Martyr, arguing for Christianity with the heathen, in about 140 A. D., says, "On the day called Sunday there is a gathering in one place of all who reside either in the cities or country places, and the memoirs of the apostles and the writings of the prophets read. We all assemble in common because it is the first day, and because on the same day Jesus Christ our Savior rose from the dead. We are circumcised from sin and error through our Lord, Jesus Christ, who rose from the dead on the first day of the week, therefore it remains the chief and first of all the days. "

Clement of Alexandria, 194 A.D., says, "The old seventh day has become nothing more than a working day."

Tertullian of Carthage, 200 A. D., says, "Sundays we give to joy, we observe the day of the Lord's resurrection, free from every hindrance of anxiety and duty, laying aside our worldly business lest we give place to the devil."

All of these men wrote from 106 to 206 years before Constantine was proclaimed emperor. They wrote before such an organization as the Roman Catholic Church was dreamed of. So, we see that the assertions of the Seventh Day people on this point are absolutely without foundation in historic fact. Even to Keep the Sabbath outside of Scripture we can trace the first day observance by Christians back to the days of the apostles.

The Seventh Day Adventists do not confine their falsifications to ancient history. They circulate far and wide that Mr. Moody has gone over to then. I have had letter after letter to this effect during the past year. This statement is absolutely false, though so often repeated. One of them deliberately circulated at a Bible School where I was teaching, last summer, that I had accepted the Seventh Day Sabbath and was going to teach it this year. Of course, this statement had not the shadow of basis in fact. I have made a study of the Sabbath question for years, and saw clearly, years ago. that Seventh Dayism had absolutely no footing in scripture. Why do they use such methods? Because, being untrue to the Word of God, they soon become untrue to other things.

Dr. R. A. Torrey

www.ingramcontent.com/pod-product-compliance
Lightning Source LLC
Chambersburg PA
CBHW031159090426
42738CB00008B/1399